MW00976963

THE EXCUSE ASSASSIN

EXCUSES

Destroying the Enemy that Stands Between You and Your Goals

Jeff Grillo

Intro

The Excuse Assassin

Destroying Your Excuses is the Only Way to a Better Tomorrow!

Jeff Grillo Media

ISBN : 9781515274179
2015

Prologue

This book has been birthed from a lifetime of knowledge and wisdom accumulated through struggles of the worst kind. Many years of my life were spent hiding my problems, or hiding my need for help because of embarrassment.

For far too long I could not deal with the idea there was something that was truly wrong with me. I felt nobody understood, and, therefore, I put up walls that I would spend much of my life hiding behind. The biggest wall was the wall of humor. I did my best to laugh away my problems.

I found myself in my mid-twenties losing my eyesight and facing several other monumental struggles that only seemed to compound the misery I was facing on a daily basis. In addition to the loss of my sight, I also went through a divorce, two forms of malignant cancer at the same time, heart problems, chronic pain and as if all that wasn't enough I faced financial ruin due to the fact I had no health insurance when

going through cancer treatment. Because I was
so confident nobody understood what I was
going through, I was not really good at
reaching out and getting help. The absence of a
mentor or other trusted friend that had
experienced even one of my challenges was
the main reason I found myself constantly in a
war to reinvent the wheel.

The stupidity of youth didn't do me any favors.
If I knew then what I know now, I would have
done everything I could to seek counsel from
others who had faced and overcame the
challenges that seemed to constantly slap me
down. Additionally, I wasn't too terribly
brilliant with the ideas and solutions I had
come up with on my own.   This, of course,
just serves to further illustrate the extreme
importance of buddying up with someone who
could have talked some sense   into me. I
understand some things can only be learned
by trial and error and personal experience, but
I contend that I could have accelerated my
triumphs over challenges far sooner had I
learned the realities of life sooner.

My intention in writing this book to you is to open your eyes, lift your chin up, and, if necessary, to do whatever it takes to get you to a full realization that you are somebody incredibly special, well-equipped and capable of not only facing challenges, but literally hunting them down, and eliminating them one by one until you stand alone atop a heap of dead lies you now call obstacles!

Table Of Contents

Intro 1

Prologue 3

Reviews 9

Know Your Enemy 12

What's the Objective? 33

Battlefield of the Mind 52

Catch the Vision 68

And...ACTION! 83

My Ultimate Secret Weapon 96

Epilogue 109

The Excuse Assassin

Destroying Your Excuses is the Only Way to a
Better Tomorrow!

Jeff Grillo Media

Reviews

"Through real-life examples of his own personal hardships and challenges, mixed with humor, Jeff lights the way for anyone who is ready to stop making excuses and reach their dreams. Written in easy to understand language, this book is filled with powerful images and stories that will ignite the soldier in anyone who is in need of motivation and a good reason to persevere. Get ready for a mix of laughter and tears that will touch your heart and inspire you to get moving in the direction of your full potential. Jeff has walked and continues to walk on a road littered with land mines, but we are blessed that he has chosen to turn around, take our hands and lead us to safety."

- Christine Bearse, Business Coach
The Goal Whisperer
www.thegoalwhisperer.com

"The Excuse Assassin by Jeff Grillo is a short read, with long term hope and encouragement. If you are feeling sorry for yourself, feel like giving up or already have, then read this book. In it you will find the story of a man faced with some of the hardest battles that a human being can be hit with, yet still finds the strength to pick himself up and not just go on with life, but embrace it. It is written from his heart to yours from both sides of life. If you are looking from the dark side, you will find that ray of light that will help you to see the hope that is reaching out its hands towards you. If you are looking from the light side, it will make you stop and take a moment to appreciate it. Either way, read it, you will find insight on how to pick yourself up, brush yourself off, and move forward no matter what you face."

- Cliff Maynard,
Success Innovations Inc.,

"...He is always so spiritually uplifting to me and my family...Jeff will always be a blessing I am thankful for."

- Robert Rozzelle, Owner
Carolina Classic Carriers

Know Your Enemy

The key foundational truth, which will be the cornerstone of the rest of this book, is to know your enemy. I mean it only makes perfect sense, right? After all, how can you fight an enemy which you have not first clearly defined?

I will use myself as the example. Unfortunately for me, there are many enemies from which I can choose. The mother of all enemies for me also happens to be the one I have had to deal with the longest-- blindness. I was diagnosed with retinitis pigmentosa (RP) when I was only five years old. There was a family history of this disease and I had been showing signs of difficulty early on in my childhood by my clumsiness I exhibited. Even though I still clearly recall many of the visits to eye doctors that were associated with the diagnosis, I cannot say for certain when it was that I was officially told of my situation and the serious impact it would have on my future. I do know that I have always had challenges with my sight. Difficulty seeing the chalkboard and reading in school were a constant thorn in my side. I did my best to hide my struggle with humor and was probably known more for being the class clown than being the guy who couldn't see well. Ah, if I only had it to do all over again! I would have gladly exchanged the laughter for some understanding and real assistance. I often wonder how my life would have unfolded differently had I been brave enough to take on the enemy of blindness, or back then just the difficulty associated with poor sight.

The best that I can recall, I was a senior in high school probably about 17 or 18 years old at the time when my parents had a discussion with me. It was this time that my parents had a serious heart to heart with me about making better choices and finding my way in a world knowing the loss of sight would continue and put me at a serious disadvantage.

I could have done much better, to say the least, to prepare myself for what was in front of me.

But sadly, I did not. Denial was a huge part of my existence for much of my life. In fact, I dedicated an entire chapter to it in my first book, "Power In Perseverance." This again, was rooted in the fact that I failed to reach out and make real connections with anyone who had already faced and overcame similar challenges. Oh, how helpful that could have been to me!

I do not want to get too far into the issues that I have gone into in my other book, so if it seems like there is more to this story than I am giving up here, it is not to be elusive. I will just point you to the other   book.
But, you do indeed know how adversely the gradual loss of my sight has been. Again, it has been for me the most formidable enemy I have had to face and overcome. Imagine for a little bit, if you can, being in my shoes. On the one hand, I was able to grasp hold of the greatest freedom any teenager ever could know, that of the obtaining of a driver's license. I will say here though, in hindsight, I really should not have ever had a license! It truly is a miracle

that I never killed myself or anyone else for that matter. By the time I was of age to drive, my sight was already bad enough that driving at night was never allowed, and I was required to wear corrective lenses during the day. This privilege of freedom was to become more of a burden at times than a joy. I became obsessed with time and weather conditions early on. It wasn't just that I had to be home by a certain time I had to be mindful of, but also of the daylight that was available day by day. Of course, it changed with weather conditions and time of year so it was a constant source of anxiety for me. Then I always needed to be aware of traffic conditions and alternate routes, just in case!

Ultimately, I lost my ability to drive on November 14, 1999. Now I live a life that in some ways is better. I mean, I no longer have the stress I used to experience associated with driving. In exchange, I now live a life of constant waiting. Let me tell you that this is not good! I am a pretty impatient person by nature and when I decide I want or need to do

15

something, it is usually right now! I guess part of my growing process included a serious need to help me learn to be more patient. I'm not all the way there, but closer than ever before. My life revolves around waiting for buses, waiting for cabs, waiting for a friend to pick me up or waiting for my wife to get home after work to take me where I need to go.

Then there is the discrimination that comes with being a person with an obvious handicap. I hate to say it because I really think that people bang the gong of discrimination a bit excessively. Well, I used to think that anyway. It is easy to think it doesn't exist when it doesn't happen to you. But when it does, it is unmistakable and painful. The most blatant instance of discrimination I experienced is awful and one that I feel I need to share with you. I was at a point in my life where my sight was poor enough I couldn't "fake it." I walked with a white cane, but had enough residual sight to see and comprehend what was going on around me better than most would assume by looking at me.

I showed up for a job interview looking sharp, wearing a very nice suit, carrying my briefcase which contained my resume and supporting documentation I may need to have on hand. In the other hand was the dreaded giveaway...my white cane. The position was for an anatomy & physiology instructor at a school that trained massage therapists. I had worked for a few years as a therapist myself when I lived in Florida and had a successful history teaching this particular course. I was well qualified for what I was there for, not to mention my extensive history in broadcasting and public speaking. They were lucky to get a guy like me for what they were offering in return!

As I approached the reception desk, I could already see a look of concern on the face of the man that sat there. I introduced myself and told why I was there and with whom I was to meet. I was told they were not there. I politely, but firmly said there must be a mistake I had an appointment and had confirmed. I saw the man dip into the office, which was presumably the interviewer's office, and whisper something. I then saw clearly he stepped back out into the hallway where I had a direct line of sight and then out popped the head of the presumed boss. She took one look at me standing there smiling with my cane in hand and she looked at the receptionist and shook her head no and motioned to get rid of me. He walked over and said sorry she is not here. At this point, I do not think I have to describe in too much detail the furious anger that rose up in me! There are many different paths I could have gone down that day. The choice was hard, but made in an instant. I wished him a nice day, turned and walked out the door and on my way. The decision I made was to not be angry and lash out. I decided I was happy they showed me up front the kind of people that they clearly were. I decided I was better than that and they did not in any way, shape or form deserve to have me work for them. This is not to say I wasn't angry. It is not to say I wasn't hurt. I simply am saying I made a decision at that moment to not allow the weaknesses of others determine my self worth, and neither should you!

There are so many other examples I can give you about how horrible the enemy of blindness is, but I think I have given you enough to get the idea. Plus, I think just about anyone can imagine the difficulties the loss of sight would present. Later on in this book, I will offer up how I took care of this particular enemy.

Cancer is one of the words in the English language that I hate the most. Just the mention of the word stirs up feelings of anger and dread. Feelings of anger because of the people I have lost in my life to this horrible disease, and all the other emotions it stirs up because of my own personal battle with two forms of the disease nearly a quarter century ago.

The enemy of cancer reared its ugly heat at a time in my life when I least could have expected it, not that I imagine anyone expects to develop cancer, but certainly not during the

19

prime of youth. I was 21 years old and had completed my first year of college. I had taken a semester off to get married. About a month prior to the wedding when I should have been starting my second semester, I discovered a rather painful, tiny bump. The nodule on one of my testicles had gotten to the point of borderline excruciating pain and after about a month of denial, it was finally time to get checked out. I was horribly shy and embarrassed about the whole thing, and truth be told, a bit squeamish about writing about it in such a public and out there kind of way today. But I feel it is not only important to the overall telling of my story, but also critical for other young men to have a certain awareness of such things. After all, it could save a life someday! So the very short version of this story leads me to share that eventually I got the diagnosis that the suspicious nodule was a tumor and that the only way to know for sure would be to do a biopsy, which meant full-blown surgery.

The surgery was a success! Once I was with it
enough and the doctor had come around, it
was explained to me that the pathologist
discovered that there was not one, but two
separate types of cancer that were growing in
the tumor and that both were malignant. In
order to preserve my life, due to the severity of
the cancers it was determined the best thing
for me was to remove the affected testicle.
Now, if you have been blessed enough to have
never had to go through surgery of any kind,
especially for cancer, allow me to tell you at
this point that this whole experience up to this
point was terrifying. Not only was my world
shattered in terms of getting the rude
awakening that mortality was for real, but the
thought that I may reach my end far sooner
than I ever could have imagined! If you ever
have gone through surgery for a serious
matter such as this, then you already know
exactly what I am talking about and can
empathize fully.

The next slap in the face was delivered a
matter of weeks later. I had recovered from

surgery and was back at work demonstrating and selling musical instruments at the mall. I was called to the office to take a phone call. It was a woman calling from the oncologist's office. I had recently had blood work done at the office and was awaiting results that I presumed I would get at my follow up visit. Imagine my horror when a concerned sounding voice confirmed that it was indeed Jeff Grillo she was talking to, then proceeded to tell me that my doctor needed to see me in his office as soon as possible. A terrible chill went through my body, as I just knew this could not be good. Within hours, I was sitting with the doctor who began to explain the results of the blood work with me. He was an amazing doctor who in my opinion, at the time, was awfully young to be in his position. While not exactly a Doogie Howser, I imagined him to be only in his 30s. At any rate, despite his seemingly young age he exuded immense confidence and competence and had a wonderful sense of humor and was just the coolest doctor ever, if I may say so. But it was at this time he explained that the cancer seemed to be indicating it was on the march. He used much different terminology, but this was the basic point. He explained due to the severity of one form of cancer in particular that I was facing only two options at this point. Option number one, I could choose to do nothing and maybe I might live up to a year! I interrupted asking, "What's option two?" He proceeded to tell me about aggressive combination chemotherapy. He said he understood it sounded scary and he wasn't going to lie it was pretty awful to endure. The glimmer of hope came when he shared this was a good idea because as awful as it was, he believed the cancer was at an early enough stage that I had a very high chance of killing this thing that was trying to kill me. Perhaps needless to say, I chose option number two!

The next couple months were indeed as awful as advertised. I lost my hair, was sick as a dog most of the time feeling very weak and ended up in the ER over and over again with serious infections due to my diminished immune system from the chemo. I even gained a ton of weight. Yeah, you wouldn't think that would be the case, but because I wasn't eating they pumped me with steroids to stimulate my appetite.

Guess what? They worked really well! I went from about 185 pounds to at times pushing 250! I went from being skinny as a rail to being a body double for the Michelin Man!

The ordeal was almost intolerable, but as it is stated in the Bible, "this too shall pass!" Eventually all things pass on. Good times, bad times, joy, sorrow, abundance, lack. Let's face it--we are in a constant state of change. I've heard it said that you are either in a crisis, coming out of a crisis, or heading into a crisis! Not necessarily comforting words, but a reality check that helps us to focus on pushing forward always! I'm not sure this will fit with the rest of this chapter, but I'm going to throw it in as a bonus. I do not read or understand the Chinese language, but have heard it said that the Chinese word for crisis is made up of two characters that are two other words. Crisis is made up of the character words: danger and opportunity.

Think about that for a moment! See how that can apply to the challenges that you face? Yes, for me, cancer absolutely was a crisis in my life, a monumental one at that. Certainly there was danger in this crisis. Obviously, I could have lost my life, or other complications could have arisen due to the surgery, such as infections or other issues. What was the opportunity? Through the passing of time, there have been so many lessons learned. Being able to grasp my mortality and learn to not be afraid of it but to   use it to propel me to strive for more has become a blessing. Also, it has lead to me writing a book and speaking to many about the ordeal. It has given me the opportunity to help so many people cope with their challenges and now I'm in the process of writing a second book, which will continue the work of helping others. Spend some time thinking how the danger/opportunity equation can work in your own personal struggles, whatever they may be.

Continuing with knowing and defining the enemies that seek to hold you back, or even destroy you if you allow them to do so, I will take you to the next major hurdle in my life. At the time of my diagnosis, I told you I was only 21 years old and in the process of getting married. I did not have any health insurance at all! I was blessed with a surgeon and oncologist that did not charge me for their services; however, there were still so many things I was still going to have to be responsible for. Hospital fees, medications and a long list of other charges left me over $100,000 in debt! It is a very, long story how I eventually got out of this situation, again I told it in detail in "Power In Perseverance," so I won't repeat it here, but in the fullness of time I did indeed eventually get out of it after several years. Suffice it to say that if your challenges are financial there is hope for you too! If a blind, uneducated (at the time), underemployed fellow can do it, so can you!

For the sake of brevity from this point, I will only hit some of the highlights that followed just to pile on a little bit. Of all my challenges in my life, I consider the loss of my eyesight and the battle with cancer to be the two biggest, hopefully never to be topped! As a result of the cancer, crushing debt, blindness and so many other factors, some my fault, some not, I ended up divorced after less than four years of marriage. I found myself a 25 year old sleeping on my grandmother's couch, newly alone and divorced. I know if you are an adult reading this book there is a better than fifty percent chance you can relate to the heartache and pain and challenges associated with going through such an ordeal. The fact that this was heaped upon everything else I already mentioned just served to further beat me down and damage my self-esteem. I suppose the best thing that came out of this experience was to be able to look back upon it and glean wisdom from mistakes made and to have understanding of what never to do again! Also, I was very thankful that we never had children. For those of you who have gone through the breakup of a family, I can't imagine your pain and heartache!

I also spent a good part of my adult life battling issues with a heart valve issues that leads to some pretty bad chest pain, usually when I least expect it. It's hard to put into words the anxiety and stress this causes. It turns out that it is essentially a benign situation, but nonetheless has lead me to big expenses at the ER. The whole being in touch with my mortality thing turned me into a bit of a chicken for many years! I found it difficult to just ignore fierce pain in the left side of my chest. I mean, what if this time I was ignoring a heart attack? Oh brother! Then there were the years of treatment for heart rhythm issues, again benign but terribly disturbing!

This is in no way a complete accounting of my life's struggles. Sometimes I think it would be a never-ending series! But, I feel that sharing these, the most significant of my challenges along the road of life, would suffice. My intention for sharing these specific ones is multi-purposed. Part of the reason I chose these were to illustrate who I am and where I am coming from through the rest of this book. I

also intend to prove that I am really nobody
special and that if I can face, live through and
overcome these formidable enemies then so
can you! Maybe, just maybe, there is also a bit
of intent to shame you! Again, I am nobody. I
don't want to shame you because I am so great
and if you aren't tough like me, then you are
somehow flawed. Nothing could be further
from the truth! My point is that I totally
understand that it is simply human nature to
sometimes allow ourselves to get into a rut.
We sometimes can find ourselves in a pity
party that probably should have lasted maybe
a day or so has turned into months or even
years!

Maybe somehow the telling of my story will
stir up something within you that cries out, "no
more!" Hey, if a guy like Jeff can shake off such
horrible things, then why can't I? That is what I
mean by shaming you into getting out of any
rut you might find yourself trapped in!

Identifying your enemy is essential. Pardon
any pun here, but until you can clearly see

your challenge, it is hard to overcome it. Physical challenges are easy to pick up on and identify. I mean, there wasn't any trouble for me to identify blindness, cancer or heart problems. Those were no brainers! I recognize other challenges we face may not be so obvious, at least not to us as we are in the middle of them. Maybe the challenge has to do with our financial situation. Well, identifying the fact that our financial situation stinks may not be too hard to see, but perhaps the reasons may be unclear. Denial can come into play and rooting out the actual cause can be a greater challenge. Maybe there is a psychological component to it. Maybe the need to feel like we are somebody leads or compels us to overspend and keep up with the Jones'? Maybe we use things to fill a certain emptiness we feel inside. Maybe we don't want to admit to ourselves that in order to improve our situation we have to do hard work like go to night school and get our GED, or take courses on the weekend at a community college, or pursue an MBA online. Maybe any one of these could be a great solution, but it becomes not so obvious to us because we refuse to kick ourselves in the backside and take action. But, please, I implore you to spend some quality time swimming in the deep end of "Lake You!" Get to the source of your challenge. Figure out what the deeper underlying challenge is and identify it! Until you get to the root of your problems, you cannot overcome them.

Now, just a quick warning before I close out this chapter, make sure you keep reading! Just in case you were inclined to finish out this chapter and ponder your challenges and take my advice to fully identify your enemy. Be careful not to allow yourself to wallow in negativity. Don't allow yourself to spend too much time dwelling on things that can further damage your self-esteem. In fact, I might suggest you hold off on taking the advice I've offered up here until you have completed the book in its entirety, especially if you are the kind of person that is inclined to self-defeatism. I would rather you read this book as a whole and get the overall point that challenges are not curses, but blessings in disguise. It really and truly is a matter of perspective. If you are a generally negative person who engages in self- defeating behavior, then please read on and hold off until you have the big picture before beginning the process of identifying your challenges. It will serve you much better.

I contend you are not a mistake. You are not an accident. I believe you are fearfully and wonderfully made. I believe you are chock full of potential and gifts. Through the reading of this book we will uncover the goodness and put you in a position to win!

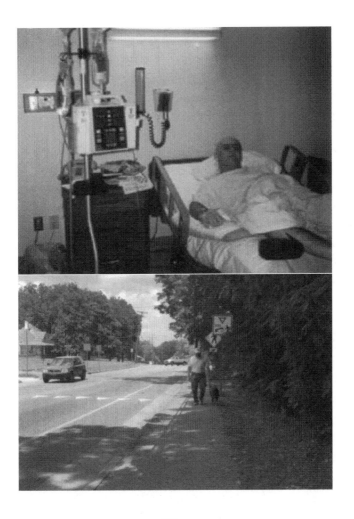

33

What's the Objective?

Well, now that the hard part is finished, we have identified our most troublesome of challenges. It is time to plot our course forward! It has been said that if you don't know where you are going, any road will get you there. I wish I knew who said that because it is so simple yet so brilliant. As simple a concept as this is though, it is remarkable how many of us simply manage to miss it. For every person, I don't care who you are, this is just a harsh fact of life. You must, without exception, have a plan or you are destined to mediocrity at best. So, for the rest of us who aren't born with a silver spoon in our mouth, or have the extreme blessed position of not having any major limitations upon us, it is all the more important that we know where we are going.

This is not going to be one of those chapters in a book that resemble a pitch from a guy trying to get you to join their multi-level marketing scheme. If you have ever been suckered into sitting through one of those meetings, you know what I am talking about. You know where the guy in the suit with all the glittering jewelry and Rolex watch stands up there asking questions like "if time and money were no hindrance to you, what would you like to be doing?" Then he goes on to show a power point presentation or guide you through a flip chart that more resembles an episode of Lifestyles of the Rich and Famous more than anything, but nowhere near reality for the 95 percent of people in the world!

Please don't get me wrong, I understand dreams. I understand motivation as well as the next guy. I believe that if you don't have a big enough dream or goal, or whatever you want to call it, you will never strive for more. I also understand the value in basing our current actions on realistic, attainable goals.
Look, I can set a goal for myself that will get me totally stoked right here right now. I can totally envision myself cutting through the waves at the helm of a Mangusta 310. At least I think that is what it was called! The yacht I am thinking of was many millions of dollars and

was top end luxury beyond my ability to explain and do it any justice whatsoever. It had a couple bedrooms, a movie theater, dining room, bar (which I would turn it into an ice cream stand) massage therapy rooms and so on. It was so big it had a staff of several people from porters, a captain and deck hands to massage therapists, chefs and the list goes on.

When I was a kid, I used to think the Grillo family was pretty well off. Somewhere in my high school years, my dad bought a 32-foot Pierson sailboat. Especially with the sails up, this thing was enormous to me.
There was enough room to sleep a family of four comfortably. There was a kitchen and a little bathroom complete with a stand up shower. In fact, I thought we were downright rich until we planned a family getaway on the boat. The destination was Newport, Rhode Island. You probably can easily jump ahead and see where I am going with this! After sailing a good part of the day, best I can recall, we arrived. I took the dingy, which sat maybe 3

of us and I puttered along on the way to shore. We floated gently past all kinds of ocean-going vessels. All along, my jaw hanging open in absolute amazement! The one private yacht that still to this day stands out in my mind was ridiculously out of this world. In addition to simply being massive, it had two twin engine Scaraab boats hanging from cranes at the stern of the ship. People like us had a rubber dingy that held 2 or 3 people and barely moved with its tiny whirring outboard motor that probably knocked out a massive 20 horsepower! Remember the opening to the old TV show Miami Vice? That cigarette boat, they call them, that was a Scaraab! These things were at least 32 foot long each and had two massive outboards each and could probably do serious speed! Additionally, this yacht was at least three levels that I could discern. Our house didn't even have three levels! Then, as if it were the crown jewel itself, sitting high atop this magnificent ship was a helicopter! Come on now! Needless to say, this was a shocking dose of reality. It was an awe-inspiring experience and humbling at the same time.

So, here's the problem in my estimation when
we dream to this extent. When the dream or
the goal is so far out there and so massive and
I'll say it, unrealistic, it puts us in a place where
we are set up for frustration and eventually
failure. And not to burst your bubble or
anything, but maybe you or even I could get
there someday. I contend that if we do, it is
because we set a whole lot of smaller, more
attainable and gradually increasing goals along
the way.

I actually had a guy probably twenty years ago
try to guilt me into getting involved in his
scheme. He played upon my losing my sight.
His pitch was "when they get to a place where
they can fix your eyes, don't you want the
money to be able to go and get it done without
having to wait longer for insurance to cover
it?" Good grief! I am as optimistic as anyone I
have ever known. In fact, I'll say it right here
right now for all the world to read, I sincerely
believe I will see 20/20 one day! Whether
through direct miraculous, divine intervention

or through the miracle of scientific breakthrough, I believe it will happen in my lifetime. No doubt. Period. End of story. My belief in this fact is unshakeable. There is also a little thing we should temper our dreams with and it is called reality. What if I had listened to that guy? Twenty years in how satisfying would it be, even if I had realized decent success in what he was peddling, there is still no cure and my miracle is still out there on the road ahead somewhere. Not to say that being prepared for such an eventuality is not a worthy goal, I mean, sure it is. But if the goal is not realistic then of what worth or what satisfaction would there be? Maybe I am wrong, but I don't think so. I just feel as though any gain that I had accrued pursuing the specific goal aforementioned would be filled with frustration and perhaps a touch of anger or resentment. At the very least, at some point during the past twenty years it would have required serious re-evaluation of goals on my part, I promise you. Without actual, tangible attainable goals, how can you keep on?

You know the obstacles that lay in front of you. Decide what is your ultimate, reasonable, attainable goal. Once you get the ultimate goal, you can break it down into smaller bite-sized attainable goals that serve as landmarks on the road to your goal. For example, let's just take my obstacle of blindness to show you what I mean. I have already in the previous chapter given you a glimpse into my world. It is a difficult, frustrating, at times embarrassing world filled with a seemingly never-ending list of things to overcome. For me, the starting point is understanding and accepting the fact. The fact was, and is still, that unless a miracle comes I am going to one day in all likelihood be in a perpetual world of total darkness. Hopefully, this diagnosis is not completely dead on correct, but as a worst-case scenario, it is where I live everyday.

Once I came to terms with this, there were some other realities I had to deal with. First and foremost, as a man, the paramount concern I have is pretty much common to all of us "manly men" types! We simply want and desire to be able to do something we love, or at least "like" and earn good wages to be able to care for our families. We want to provide a nice, safe and secure home. We want enough food on the table. We would like to be able to take off a little quality time each year with the family. We want to have reliable transportation, healthcare coverage, a little retirement plan going, oh yeah, and be able to at least help significantly with our children's college. That doesn't seem like much in the sense it is just common everyday stuff we all think about and do our best to plan. That is until you start to break it down and realize the average, decent new car is in the mid $20,000 range and up. The cost of food is crazy on the rise. An average home is upwards of $150,000 and that's if you pay cash. If you take out a mortgage, it is something like more than double that by the time you pay it off!

Just making it through to retirement is daunting enough for anyone, much less with a monumental challenge like blindness! So, now that I had come to terms with my situation and realize that my general, basic human needs and desires are still the same as anyone, what am I to do? There are a few roads I can take, and the same probably applies to you, although perhaps in different ways. I could say woe is me! What a horrible lot in life, I guess I'll just sit down and shut up and take whatever I can get. By this I mean, I can apply for social security disability and figure out a way to exist for the rest of my life on whatever the all-compassionate government representatives determine is what I am worth. For most in my situation, that probably ranges from a low around $600 per month to somewhere up to around $1,800 a month, maybe.

Now if a person is so lucky as to be at the high end of that spectrum and also have a spouse earning a living that may be pretty close to a tolerable existence as long as the spouse does pretty well. But what kind of life is that? What self worth would you have? Dreams would be out of the question because you would be at the mercy of whatever annual increases you might get as long as Congress agreed there was either a way or the will to give it.

There are probably other options on the table, but this is not an exhaustive dissertation on all the ways for a blind man to make a living! The other way that I could go is to come up with a realistic "vision" of myself. I could match what I like to do and can do well with how to turn that into an income. If I chose a line of work that essentially was computer based I could then begin to look at the normal path, educationally speaking, to reach that goal. I might want to think about sitting down with counselors at potential schools where I could acquire the training necessary to achieve the goal. I then could talk with the person on campus in charge of assisting those with disabilities and discuss the reality of whether or not the education could be achieved and with the current technology available whether or not I could get the work done in the classroom and then in the field. The next question I would need to ask is am I the first guy who is blind to try to do this kind of work?

43

If not, then there is great hope for me! Any time someone like yourself has achieved a goal you are interested in, the probability of you being able to achieve it too go up greatly! What if there is nobody known at the time that has done it? Nothing wrong with being a pioneer as long as you are ok with that!

With hard work and determination, you can be confident that you can achieve the certification necessary. Why not? Go for it. As for me in pursuit of my goals, I have had many satisfying moments tempered with a whole lot of, well, not so good results! But I have a great tenacious side to me, and I suggest you go ahead right now and adopt that kind of spirit for yourself! It may be what it takes as much as any gifting or skill.

The fact that you are reading this book now is proof I am chugging on down the road and fulfilling my life dreams and goals one day at a time. This is my second book, and I already have a third that will come out soon. Technically, it was my second, but I felt strongly to put it on the back burner even though I'm only a chapter or so from finishing it. Eventually it will come out! Maybe you have discovered my blog that shows it's read the world over. Maybe you have subscribed to or at least listened to an episode of my weekly podcast where I offer up healthy and meaningful doses of encouragement, motivation and inspiration.

Maybe you watched some of my YouTube videos that offer up the same encouragement? Or perhaps, you have sat in a room with others and listened to me share-uplifting words of wisdom from a stage or pulpit?   I am not cruising the Mediterranean on my Mangusta, not yet at least. I am not sure I ever will do that because my priorities are much different today than they were twenty years ago. If I had millions to buy a boat, I'd probably pay someone to slap me silly prior to giving it away to help others. Yes, I get paid for what I do. That is satisfying in and of itself, but far more satisfying is the fact that I found a way to fulfill my divine purpose on this earth. One area of my life I work diligently towards is sharing the

Gospel and building the Kingdom of my Messiah. On the other side, I do the other things I do to offer up encouragement, motivation and inspiration to hurting, frustrated people like I used to be.

That was my goal. I never want to be that guy on TV preaching a different gospel that revolved around shaking down the faithful for money so I could live the good life. No, thank you! That is not me. I always seek to do all that I can do in that arena so I can reach the ultimate success plan one day, in Heaven. But, there are the realities of this world and I need to earn a living, so in a separate capacity altogether, I have found a way that works for me, earns me a living, but still offers far more value to the end user than I will ever receive this side of eternity. For me, that's just the way I like it!

The greater question in front of us now is, what about you? What is your objective? How can you, with whatever obstacles you face, achieve the goals to making a life that everyone else desires, too? Just because people like you and me face challenges of many different kinds does not make us all that different when it comes right down to it. We are still human with the same beating hearts, desires and needs as everyone else. The only real difference is that, for whatever reason, we have to work longer and harder to make it happen. I contend that I firmly believe there is nothing wrong with that. The greater the struggle, the greater the reward. That does not always translate into dollars and cents, but it does translate into dignity and self-worth! These are commodities far more valuable in my thinking than anything I can invest in on Wall Street!

Another piece of advice that is fitting for this chapter on setting your objectives is in alignment with preparation. It is my humble opinion that it is a fantastic idea to surround yourself with good, reliable counsel that has your best interests at heart. If you are married, then your spouse is hopefully your number one go to on this one! If you are a churchgoer

than you'd better involve your Pastor or Rabbi
in on this one. Then, of course, get the counsel
of advisors at the school, if that is necessary
for you to reach your goal or seek counsel of
one who has gone through what you are facing
today. Listen to the advice each one offers up.
Ask them what they think you're good at
doing. You may be surprised that what they
say is in complete agreement with hidden
goals or desires you may have had! You may
also be surprised to find their answers in stark
contrast with them! Either way, listen closely
and as best you can, objectively listen to what
they say. Again, if you are the praying type, this
is also a great time to seek the ultimate counsel
of the Father! At any rate, seek the highest
counsel in your life and what is most
important to you.

Once you have set your clear objectives, be
certain to set up accountability. Don't worry, if
higher education is part of the plan, grades
and professors will do a phenomenal job at
keeping you accountable! If your path does
not include this route, surround yourself with

the type of people I mentioned earlier and check-in with them regularly to keep yourself on track. It may sound silly, or perhaps even a bit juvenile, but trust me, it is essential.

Don't be afraid to adjust your course! Some of the best thought out plans that the world has ever seen have sometimes been blown off course and into unexpected territory before realizing ultimate success. To go back to the boating example, I apparently am fond of, you can sit on the dock with your charts and plot out a course to an island somewhere you want to visit. That's not too tough for someone who knows what they are doing. But the seas, and life itself, have an amazing capacity to throw surprises at you often.

When relying on sails to catch the wind, as opposed to a gas engine, you are particularly vulnerable to changing conditions. A sudden unforeseen change in the direction of the wind can cause you to have to head in a completely different direction than you had originally planned. You have to travel in a new direction in order to position yourself to take advantage of the new conditions and eventually pilot your vessel to the intended destination. This change in winds, and subsequent change in course, may end up taking you more time and have you covering more distance than you had intended; it may even have you end up far more worn out than you imagined, but if you act smartly, continue with the end in mind, you can eventually turn things in your favor. There is something so sweet about being able to adapt and compensate for unforeseen adversity. In life, it is probably a statistical guarantee that at some point you will face adversity. The sooner you can compensate and adapt an altered course, the faster you can arrive at the place you wanted to go in the first place! The longer you hesitate or waiver or simply fail to make the effort to change you will drift farther and farther off course until time or supplies, in the case of sailing, make it impossible to reach your goal. Life can be that way, too. We only have so long until our number is called, so-to-speak. The longer we waste time unable to cope with a change in course brought on by unexpected adversity, the less likely we are to correct back to our original plan. If, and or when, this happens we are closer, dangerously so, to being forced to accept less than we wanted for ourselves, our families and those who are counting on us!

Decide where you want to go. Assess what it takes to get there. Surround yourself with those who can help you in one capacity or another to achieve that goal. Be diligent and press towards the goals no matter how you feel. Be willing to adjust your sails when adversity comes. Expect it and be ready for it. Be sharp and on your guard to detect when you are off course. The quicker you can adjust, the better for you! You can and will, if you choose, achieve the dignity and self-respect that pursuing and attaining your goals will bring.

...... of the Mind

In the first two chapters of this book, you have learned to identify your enemy and set clear objectives so that you may have what you need to get the job done. On occasion, you may find that it is not too terribly difficult to accept all that was taught in the first two chapters. Most of us understand our situations. Sure, some of us reside in an area of life where our zip code indicates we are smack dab in the middle of denial! But, by and large, most of us get it. Having clear objectives is something many of us can, with a little guidance, grasp pretty well. But, for far too many of us, the real trouble sets in where the rubber meets the road. Now that the problem is identified and you have a plan all we have to do is get rolling, right? It shouldn't be too hard to do. Alas, getting the hind end in gear can be trickier than one would think.

I believe it was mentioned in the previous chapter and bears repeating here. Be careful once you have set your goals! It is a natural thing to set our eyes on the ultimate goal. It is good to be able to "see" yourself walking in your own personal victory, whatever that may look like. In fact, I will get to vision here momentarily. The problem is not in the imagining of a totally successful you. The problem can sometimes creep in when we allow ourselves to get wrapped up in the enormity of the future you. Here's a concept I have to take by faith nowadays, but if our goal is a mountaintop many miles in the distance, we can look and see it clearly. The trouble with seeing the mountaintop clearly is that everything that is right in front of us is blurry and indiscernible. Likewise, when we try to look into the future and take a peek at who we believe in our hearts we were supposed to be, the smaller initial steps can become blurred and we find ourselves in a state of indecision and fear can set in. This indecision and fear can ultimately lead to inaction. Inaction, of course, keeps us firmly cemented in the here and now, and again with the passing of time makes the ultimate goal increasingly more difficult to achieve.

Within our precious, little heads a war rages!
There are voices doing battle all the time.
Please understand I am not a psychologist or
psychiatrist or in any way a mental health
professional. That is my official disclaimer! I
believe the voices I am talking about are
normal. I'll state it here that if the voices you
hear are telling you to do bad, harmful or evil
things, seek help immediately! For the rest of
us, these voices play out in the form of self-
conversation. We "talk out" decisions that are
to be made, things to do and so many other
things. For me, one of my most common
mental conversations revolves around me
contemplating decisions that need to be made.
I do my best to think out every possible
scenario that I can think of ever coming up. I
do this in order to prepare myself for what my
responses will be for different situations. I also
try to figure out what the worst possible
outcome could be and weigh whether or not
the potential benefits are better than potential
disaster that may come. Hopefully, I am
correct in my assumption that this is pretty
normal, otherwise, I'm sure I'll get a visit from

the men dressed in white coats chasing me with those giant butterfly nets! Not too hard to catch a blind man! I'm not too fast and my evasion skills are lacking.

These voices can be constructive and helpful. We just need to be on guard and exercise discernment when deciding which voices are good, true and worthy to be heeded. If we give ear to the wrong voice, the battle can be lost pretty quickly. Some of those voices sound a lot like us, but have been planted by our detractors and people that never had our best interests at heart. Voices of school bullies, or the kid who thought it was cool to be the class comedian and trash everyone around him to make himself look and feel better can rise up even in adulthood. We can be lured into thinking, maybe they're right. Maybe I am a loser. Maybe I am good for nothing. Maybe I should just sit down and shut up and accept my lot in life.

Stop! When you find yourself, even for a moment, entertaining such mental conversations, it is time to tune them out!

This concept may sound goofy or childish, but there is merit to it. I am guilty of finding humor in it, too. In fact, I flash back to the Saturday Night Live bit with Stuart Smalley. You know the one? I just remember this airy, positive talker sitting in front of a mirror repeating his mantra, "I'm good enough, I'm smart enough and doggone it, people like me." A hilarious bit to say the least., and if we do it in the style and manner Mr. Smalley did it we might find ourselves laughing and not taking it seriously. But there is a lot of merit to it, especially if done correctly and at the right time and in the right way.

When the voice pops into my head telling me there is no way I will be able to do this or that, I retort as quickly as I can with something like, "yes, I can." I am quick to point out to myself that past performance is no guarantee of future results! I remind myself that I am not the first in my situation to face and overcome a particular challenge so therefore if it has been done, it can be one, and I am next!

Sometimes tenacity and determination go a very long way to winning the battle of the mind. I try to have a pit bull mentality when it comes to killing off self-defeating negative talk. In fact, I take it further than that even. I guard my space carefully. I do not allow negative people and naysayers to get too close to me. I refuse to allow that to be part of my life anymore; I spent too many years surrounding myself with negative, sarcastic friends I used to think were funny. Now, these types of people used to make me angry enough that I kept them at a distance. Setting up that outer perimeter of safety helps you to take care of the close quarter battles that are occurring within your mind. Whatever you do, do not allow your mental enemies to get reinforcements! Now that would be a crazy thing to do! In fact, you ought to be doing the exact opposite. Fill your outer perimeter with "friendlies." The more you surround yourself with loving, positive people that have your best interests in mind, the better it will be for you.

Remember that these negative voices will always be there to some extent. Choose which voices you will feed. It is only natural to think and understand that what you feed will live and hang around, while the thing you starve will leave in search of food elsewhere. Don't entertain the negativity. Feed the positive.

How?

For me, my number one source and my main source is the Bible. I love what it has to say about me! Sure, it points out loud and clear that I am sinful and contrary to goodness by nature. Wait a minute--where are you going with this? Settle down, I haven't gone off the rails of my point. The totality of the book, well, the collection of sixty-six books to be more precise paints a beautiful picture that shows me, despite my flaws, how dearly I am loved. It lets me know I am loved, cared for, wanted,

fought over and precious enough to die for!
Say what you will, but for me this is an
enormous source of a self-esteem boost! This
basic message flies in the face of what the
world tries to convince us of every single day.
I'll take what the Bible says about me any day
over that. As a secondary source, I love to find
stories of men and women who exhibit an
extraordinary spirit and a will to survive and
overcome challenges they are faced with; it is
not always physical or mental. Sometimes they
must simply dig deep to overcome junk that
just seems to happen to them.

I don't know if the series is still on Netflix or
not, but I used to love the program called, "I
Shouldn't Be Alive." Sounds like a negative
title, Jeff! The whole premise of the show was
depicting ordinary people who suddenly found
themselves in overwhelming circumstances
that literally tested their ability to survive. You
think you have troubles, you ought to watch an
episode or two of this show. You will quickly
see that we are generally capable of so much
more than we could ever imagine. The hero in

all of us typically does not shine until we are tested. Instead of looking at your challenge, even if it is physical or emotional, as a bad thing maybe it is time to change perspective and look at it as your opportunity to show the world the hero you are!

One of my favorite episodes had to do with a fairly young man who had gone through divorce and all sorts of loss in his life. In order to cope and "find himself" he hopped aboard his sailboat and sailed across the Atlantic. Many of the details are now escaping me but the general gist of the story should be in tact! I believe it was on his return trip while his vessel was on autopilot and he slept during the night that a storm kicked up. The swells were colossal. He found himself struggling against an enemy he couldn't possibly win against-- that of nature. A massive wave hit the boat, snapping his mast and flipping his boat upside down. He frantically swam underwater trying to get whatever survival gear he could and get to his life raft before the boat sank, dragging him to a watery grave! The story goes on to show that when the storm passed and daylight came he found himself adrift far outside any shipping lanes with little to no chance of being found. He only had a few days supply of food and water he was able to grab. I want to say his entire ordeal lasted something crazy like 74 days and that may be the title of the episode, "74 Days at Sea." Against all odds, he ultimately floated to the Caribbean and was found barely alive, but alive. He survived! There are so many tales of what he did to survive, but what I found most fascinating was the mental battle he had to fight every single minute of those 74 days. It was relentless. He was surrounded by water, but it was water he could not drink. It was hot, lonely and scary. His raft was punctured by some sort of swordfish or something and he had to battle to patch it and keep afloat his tiny raft. This is a mental battle none of us will likely ever face. The intensity of this battle rivals that of any actual war I would imagine.

Although, I would rather be in the type of war this man found himself in where there were at least no bullets flying my way! I'm fragile that way, I guess.

This man exemplified what I mean when I talk about how we must battle the negative voices, shut them up and shut them down. We must battle with everything that is within us to silence them and not allow this enemy to gain any ground against us. Even as delirium from severe dehydration set in, this man was absolutely relentless in waging attack and counterattack against overwhelming odds and voices that were seemingly unquenchable.

I want you to take away a couple things from my retelling of this amazing story. First, it ought to give us hope. Like I said, you and I will hopefully never face a physical emergency in our lives that can compare to the ferocity of this one. The fact though that such a young man did face and overcome it shows us the amazing power of our minds if we simply make the right choices and shut down the negative voices.

Secondly, you need to take away the fact that simply refusing to give up can be your best asset in time of war. Adopt a pit bull type of tenacity when it comes to getting through a situation. For me, I refuse to let anyone tell me no, especially myself! I can be rude and tell myself to shut up all day long, and often do! There is no way I am going down like that, I say. There is no way I'm not going to be able to do something. Sometimes I need a little help, but I am able to do so much, it amazes even me. I have flown an airplane.

Yes, that's right! I went up with a flight instructor who knew of my background when I was a teen and my dad had an airplane. He, the instructor, followed me around the plane and guided me through the pre-flight check. When it was time to fly, I headed for the passenger seat and was quickly corrected and ordered to take the pilot seat! After some instruction, I started the engine, taxied down the runway and positioned the plane for take off. The instructor called out some stuff on the radio and told me to hit it! I throttled up the engine and when we hit the proper speed the instructor called out, "Roll out!" I pulled back on the yoke and we soared up higher and higher! I flew around the beaches of St. Petersburg, Florida. Pretty amazing for a guy who wasn't allowed to drive a car! I could see enough to get the general picture of what was going on on the instrument panel! I also could get the general picture of what was going on outside the plane, but not too good. The instructor kept asking me if I could see the two helicopters that were below and to my left. Nope! I figured as long as he could see them though, I was in pretty good shape! After my time was nearly up, he had me reduce altitude and line up with the runway. My fun was over! He took over control of the plane for landing and explained his desire to continue living! I understood and respected that goal of his, as it was mine as well!

I learned to scuba dive in the Caribbean and have been to a depth of about 113 feet below the surface. I have been at the controls of both powerboats and sailboats, even when I could not see to drive a car. I have been up in a World War II fighter plane during an airshow in the Caribbean because I pursued my dream of being a radio personality and, in doing so, was at the right station at the right time. I have been the host of a weekly dance party on the radio, which was heard on FM and AM radio stations in three or four US states, as well as on stations in Peru, Costa Rica and the rest of Central and South America via Cable Connection! When my first book came out, I had the privilege and honor of having my book go places I have still never been! I did a series of four TV interviews on Christian television that have aired literally around the world to over 100 nations! My blog, which is fairly new, has already been read and shared in 21 nations.

How am I, someone I still contend am nobody special, get the opportunity to do so much and impact so many? I refuse to give up. I do my best to be a man in motion. When I fail, and it is more often than I care to think about, I don't let it get me down. Like Thomas Edison, I don't look at the ten thousand failed attempts as failure, but as learning ten thousand ways what I was trying to do won't work. Keep trying.

Pick yourself up, dust yourself off and go and do it again and again until you get where you need and want to go.

I would be telling a giant lie if I said I never entertain the negative voices. Sure, there have been times that the enemy of negativity has gained ground on me. In fact, there have been a lot of gains by the enemy over the course of my life. What made the difference? I just jumped back into the fight as fast as I could. Sometimes that meant within minutes, other times within days or even weeks. But I got back up and got back in. I love what the great speaker Zig Ziglar used to say. "When life knocks you down, land on your back. Because if you can look up, you can get up!" See, even then it is a matter of perspective. It is hard not to have a downcast spirit with your nose is in the dirt! Lying on your back, looking up at the vastness of creation in all its splendor and beauty we realize how small we are and there is something so much bigger at work. Properly placed hope and perspective supplies a whole lot of strength when you think you cannot go on. I may not have the strength I need, but I know I can call upon the Father in Heaven to help me up. There are no bigger set of shoulders in all the universe! I'll always be more than happy to have that source to rely upon and ask for a little help getting back up and back on track.

Catch the Vision

In this chapter, I want to share a concept that I specifically used while undergoing chemotherapy. I can't honestly say for sure what contribution it made to my successful outcome for a type of cancer that simply does not have survivors. I offer up no studies or hard evidence. I only offer you two facts.

First, the principle I tapped is Bible based.

Secondly, I am alive today, more than twenty years after completing my therapies. I simply submit for your consideration what   follows.

There is a famous Bible verse that states, "without a vision, the people perish." There are different applications we can take away from this verse. For the purposes of this book, I am certainly not going to dive deep into theological meaning and debate. I just want to share two practical points that I learned in the school of hard knocks, as they say.

It is this very verse that should add great weight to the reason so many others and I place an emphasis on having a goal or set of goals. It is this vision of yourself, or future you, that keeps us alive and brimming with enthusiasm, zeal and excitement for life. It is this defining and holding on to a particular vision that motivates us and keeps us focused in a direction that holds purpose so that we don't wander aimlessly through life, getting nowhere and accomplishing nothing. For those of you who are heaven-minded, the implications are even greater and eternal as opposed to the temporal and fleeting things of this world.

The second point is actually my main one for the purposes of my story and, even more specifically, this chapter.

I'll explain it this way in the retelling of part of my cancer story. I recall the very first day I checked into St. Joseph's Cancer Institute in Tampa, Florida. I knew up front my initial stay was to be five days. The overall plan was nine to twelve weeks of aggressive combination chemotherapy. My treatments were broken down into three-week cycles. Week one had me inpatient receiving pretty intensive and seemingly constant IV drips of various drugs for the duration of the five days. Then on weeks two and three I was to be treated with other drugs two days per week. The whole thing repeated until I was done. This was their intention anyway. The reality was, however, I spent most of what turned out to be eight weeks total mostly inpatient, as almost every time I went home I would get one infection or another and be back at the ER and admitted.

Let's go back to my check-in experience. I still to this very day can feel some of the same feelings I felt that first day. When I think about it, it's almost like I'm there all over again, that is how much this experience affected me. I was so scared, to put it bluntly. I literally felt like a dead man walking. I just did not know when my death sentence might be carried out. I was scared, stressed out, I felt all alone and completely without a clue as to what I really should expect. I set my duffle bag down and was somewhat glazed over as a nurse by the name of Val helped me settle in. She seemed like the gentle, grandmother-type. I am not saying she was elderly, just that was the impression of a 21-year old, wet behind the ears, young adult had at the time. I was doing my best to listen to what she was telling me, but I was literally and physically trembling with fear all over and fighting back tears. Val was great! Clearly, she had been through this rodeo more than a few times. She clearly saw through the facade I was presenting down to the scared-to-death kid behind the exterior. She sat me down and gave me a hug telling me everything would be ok. I told you the emotions still are so fresh in my mind all these years later; I really do my best not to entertain them. But even now as I write this, I am tearing up and beginning to cry as I relive this moment for you. Her compassion, love and absolutely amazing bedside manner brought me comfort even though her words caused the dam to break and the tears really let loose at that moment! After a couple of moments, I got a grip and did my best to laugh it off and get about getting ready for the first IV to be inserted and get the first of the drugs into my system.

I remember laying there in bed, tucked in and watching while another nurse set the bag of liquid medicine and got the meds flowing. I recall the warm and mildly burning sensation as it hit my veins for the first time. I fought back the tears and did my best to smother the fear inside and move forward. It was sometime this first day that I began for some reason to have a memory of my grade school days when I used to play intramural basketball. Somehow I had been selected as co-captain of the team. Clearly, one of the earliest victims of social promotion on record! I had no business playing the game, much less having any sort of authority or leadership role at that time. Nonetheless, it was the case. I remembered the coach helping us young guys how to dribble and shoot. I remember him telling us about a thing called visualization. He told us how even the pros would stand at the free throw line, dribble, focus on the net and visualize the ball going into the net. I'm pretty sure at the time, I did my best, and perhaps the coach's visualization technique helped me improve somewhat, but I assure you as the day is long that I never amounted to anything other than a good laugh on the court!

At any rate, here I was years later in a hospital bed beginning the fight of my life. And for some reason, I was taken back to a time and place where I was taught a principle I had never used since the day it was taught. Being in a somewhat desperate situation, I began to give it more and more thought. I was a Christian, although I was a pretty weak one at the time and lacked the deep rooting that I sure could have used back then. To top it off, I had several well-meaning fellow believers in my life that told me I was making a huge mistake by taking chemotherapy. I was blasted for a lack of faith that Jesus would heal me. I was feeling pretty condemned and messed up, quite frankly, over the whole thing. Call me crazy or call me brilliant, it makes no

73

difference now, but the choice was made with the logic I could muster up that I needed to take the chemo. It was the only tangible way out I could see. I prayed for divine healing, of course. But I was also wise enough at that point to know that the Father of all creation created   doctors and is the source of all wisdom and knowledge and that had to include medicine! That's what I thought then, and is what I believe today!

I tried to think of how the whole visualization thing could apply to the situation I found myself. I had no idea where to start, so I did the best I could. I was no doctor, but I remembered the drawings in high school of cells and of peering through a microscope at various types of cells. I really had no idea what cancer cells looked like, but I did hear them referred to at one point in the past as "ugly, malformed cells." I closed my eyes and prayed for healing, I prayed for the miraculous to happen and trusted somehow, with my   life being in His hands it would all work out just fine. At least I did my best to be that rock. I began to imagine as best I could ugly, malformed cells all over my body, floating in my blood and so on. I visualized the drugs going into my arm and every time they came into contact with one of the ugly guys, the ugly guy died! I had plenty of time to kill during my treatments. While I did not maintain a constant mental movie of the drug-induced cancer slaughter, I did think upon it often. Over and over I would focus on this, seeing as though it was the only positive I could latch onto at this point, until I would fall asleep. In the hospital, you are constantly being awakened for this test or that test, this reading or that reading, so there were plenty of fall-asleep opportunities to do this exercise.

Another Scripture that came into mind was from Proverbs 23:7 that tells us, "as a man thinks in his heart, so he is." I got the whole vision thing and was doing my best to be the best little visualizer you ever did see. I did also know and have a decent understanding that lesson which was taught by Solomon in Proverbs. I knew that if I dwelt upon death, dying, sickness, etc., well, I would continue to be sick and perhaps eventually this awful disease would get the best of me and I would succumb to its devastation. If that was true, then the opposite would have to also be true. If I dwelt upon the chemo drugs winning and cancer cells losing, if I envisioned myself beating this thing and my healthy cells getting stronger and functioning perfectly, and latched onto life and health and being well, then eventually I would have to line up in the physical realms to what the Scripture says.

I cannot say that I was from this point in a constant state of peace and bliss. I cannot say that fear did not rear its ugly head here and there. I do not know of anyone who is a constant rock always, one hundred percent of the time. Do you? I would like to meet that person. I may fall down. I may even fall down repeatedly over time. I contend the thing that makes the difference from the person who is defeated and the person who is the victor is that the person who eventually wins is the guy who keeps getting up over and over despite his injuries. It kind of conjures up images of the Rocky movies. Who doesn't love those amazing films? Picture the climactic fight scenes. It doesn't really matter which move, ultimately they are all kind of the same, aren't they? But we keep watching them, why? We all love a winner. We all love when the underdog keeps going, refuses to give up and against all the odds, pulls out an amazing win in the end. That's what it is all about in those movies, and really what it should be all about in our daily lives. So you look at the ring and you have two guys going at it with all they have within them. One guy gets the upper hand and beats the hero, Rocky, senseless. He falls down over and over but despite a closed-up, bloody eye and disorientation, he gets up and gets back at it. Eventually a lucky shot gets through and connects temporarily stunning the opponent. Seizing on this unexpected opportunity, Rocky newly energized by the hit, unleashes everything he has. With each punch, the opponent is further thrown off balance and the champ is further strengthened from deep within. Back and forth the momentum of the

77

fight shifts until finally tenacity pays off and the knockout punch is delivered and the underdog is victorious!

This is why we need a vision in our life, a goal for our future. We need to know who we are, what we have to do, where we are going and who we want to be when we get there. When we have a vision that is clearly defined, we are set up for success. When trials come, and they will, I assure you they will, you will draw from the well of strength placed inside of you in order to fight whatever challenge is thrown your way. You will visualize yourself fighting and winning the battle against that obstacle. You will visualize yourself coming out the other side of the ordeal you face stronger and closer to your dreams and goals than you were when you started. You will understand that you are not alone or weird or unusual, because you understand the Biblical principle that we endure nothing except that, which is common to man. Therefore, if our challenges are common, and others have overcome them in one way or another, then so can we. We will understand our thoughts control our destiny and that as we think in our hearts, so we will be. Because we know that we will make conscious decisions to hold our focus not on the negative reports of doctors, or anyone else for that matter. We will make the choice and stick to it that we will only think on those things, which are good, pure, and of good report. We will only think of ourselves fighting and winning and not entertain "what ifs" that are inextricably attached to defeatism.

Whether you realize it or not, you are indeed a soldier on a mission. You have been placed down here in a foreign land, charged with fulfilling your purpose and overcoming whatever obstacles, snares and traps the enemy plants out there for you. You must identify, recognize and target your enemy. You must not allow your enemies we call challenges to trap you and hold you back from achieving your objectives. You will use your intellect, your emotion and your will to plan and then execute that plan to overcome your challenges. You will look to your friends and family in the fight with you for support and tap into their intelligence they have gathered. You will run the race that has been set before you. You will complete the mission and one day you will receive due compensation.

I recommend you keep this book. You should re-read it in whole or in part from time to time. Allow it to encourage you. Allow it to inspire you and if necessary give you the swift kick in the pants everybody needs from time to time. Believe it or not, even guys like me get tired. The conflicts we face are lifetime battles sometimes. Even I have to remind myself from time to time that I need to practice what I preach and yes, I give myself my own kick in the pants.

Life is so precious. I learned during my fight against cancer a valuable lesson. Well, I learned many valuable lessons, but one in particular I want to share now is the fact of how extremely fragile life is. Everyone gets it, we know we are mortal beings. Most of us, however, do our best to put that away in the deep recesses of our minds. It is not something pleasant that any of us really care to think about. But I had the great honor of learning this lesson early in life. I came to understand long ago that any day, at any time, for any reason I could find myself standing before the Almighty. That's pretty serious business, don't you think? Even in the best of scenarios, of which I firmly believe I am in, it is still a pretty overwhelming proposition. For me, it is the measuring and weighing of things in that light that not only offer me perspective, but also keep me moving. I realize even if we live a full hundred years, that is not very much time. It is here today and gone tomorrow. I have a vivid memory of when I was about five years old. I was standing in the bank with my mom and I was upset because I couldn't see over the counter. "I just want to be big." About four decades later, having two wonderful children of my own now I find myself teaching them the lesson I learned from that. Don't wish away your life. It passes so quickly all on its own, whether you think so or not. Get a vision or goal for you in your business, your family, your ministry, your conquest or your biggest challenge. See yourself winning. Keep proper perspective and keep moving.

And...ACTION!

Alright, you have survived this far, now you are pretty much in the home stretch! Whatever you do, do not quit on me.

I believe that if I just ended this book with the last chapter, that I would have given you quite enough information and shared experiences to make a vast difference in your life. I could rest and hang my hat on the fact that all of my struggles in life were not for nothing. They would have culminated in what will hopefully be a massive audience of people hungry and even a little desperate for more in their lives. I could be pretty satisfied that in some way, great or small, I have made a difference and left my mark on this crazy upside-down world we live in today. I could sit on my front porch and gaze heavenward dreaming of each of you and the positive change that has entered each heart and transformed it into something better than you were before you grabbed hold of hope offered up in these pages.

All of this would be, and quite frankly is, a wonderful set of thoughts. Not that I'm some superhero or overachiever or anything, but it is still not good enough. No, it is not good enough for me to leave you here. Even though, whether you realize it or not, we have come a long way in just a few short chapters. But there is still a couple of critical pieces to the puzzle which I must cover in order for me to truly be satisfied with what I am sincerely trying to do here through the pages of this book. You see, to me, this is not just a book. It is not an avenue by which I intend to draw income or build an empire. It is not written with the intention of gratifying my ego or of checking off an item on a bucket list. It is far more than any of that. In fact, I am positive at this point is far more than even I could have imagined.

This book, in a sense, is a window or portal if you will. Because my current intention is to release this book, at least for a time, solely in e-book format. So it really is a window of sorts. I'm on one side of your screen writing, pouring out my soul to you, and you are on the other

84

side of my screen reading and peering through the window into my life and we are linking up that way. This connection hopefully does not end simply with the transaction that occurred when you purchased and downloaded this book. It hopefully does not end when you finish the final words in the epilogue. It is my sincere hope that these things were merely a brief starting point, which becomes the genesis of relationship. No, I'm not weirding out on you, I understand it would be pretty impossible for thousands upon thousands (hopefully) of readers and I to become close buddies. Perhaps some will. What I am referring to is more a welcoming of you into a sort of community. Hopefully, you have learned enough that you desire more of what I have to offer. Perhaps this book inspires you to join my Throttle Up Network that can be found on my website and will be easily found in the links section of this e-book, or in print form at the end of the book down the road at some point. Maybe through this book you will have discovered my blog, podcast and YouTube channels, also found on the links page. I hope that maybe you'll even reach out and post a review and give a rating on the site where you purchased this book. I would also hope that at some point you decide to drop me a little note via email or comment on one of my forums and conversation is sparked. Maybe one day you'll even attend a conference where I am speaking.

With all that being said, I want to cover the material intended for this chapter. Consider this long introduction to this chapter as a freebie, a little something extra from me to you!

All the knowledge in the world is beautiful and beyond the ability of any one person to place proper value upon it. All the most stirring and compelling motivation and insights are of immense value as well. The connection between author and reader through the sharing of personal struggles and triumphs are so very special. All of these things, however, are ultimately useless to you as an individual if you fail to learn and implement this supremely important piece of the puzzle. That piece is the dirty, little word every procrastinator hates with a passion, and that word is..."ACTION!"

To the tender ones that may be reading this, I apologize for such abrasive use of the six-letter word I just used! This word has tripped up many a well-intentioned soul. It has littered cemeteries all over the world with lives that have passed from this Earth and wound up in a grave that is now filled up not only with human remains, but are filled up with the potential that was placed within them and sadly never realized. Regardless of what you may think about the meaning of life, or what happens to us when we die, the thought of wasted potential is immense beyond even our own lives. What potential are you harboring that thus far you have not taken action and unleashed in the world? What are the fruits of this potential that have been kept out of your family's reach? What neighborhood could you have lived in had you taken action? What college could you have sent your children to had you tapped into your potential and taken real, decisive action? What parts of this beautiful world could you have visited had you only acted upon what was hidden away inside of you? What charities could you have helped out financially and with your sweat and tears had you had the freedom to get involved with, but did not because you never got passed the dream and got to work to achieve it? I could go on and on with these types of questions. Spend a few moments to get in touch with the ones here that are specific and relevant to your own personal   situation.

Think of ones that I haven't mentioned but are colossally important to you. Get in touch with that awful feeling. I had a whole lot of time thinking about these things myself. If you haven't yet thought of any of these ideas, I'll give you a preview...it is horrible!

It is ok to feel horrible, just for a moment though! Don't dwell on these thoughts too much, just enough to give you a taste of the negative consequences of inaction. Think on it just enough to allow these thoughts to be one more set of tools in your toolbox to help you feel another kick in the pants and propel you into that dirty, little six letter word too many fear--action.

But, Jeff, what if I take action and still fail? I'm going to sound crass here for a second. My answer is a resounding, so what? A cheesy saying popped into my mind from my younger years when I was still a teen and had a broken heart over some now forgotten girl. My mom looked me in the eye, more than once and said something to the effect of, "better to have lived and loved, than to have never loved before." I have a feeling I butchered that saying a little bit. But, you get the point, I am sure.   To that end with respect to the premise of the question "what if I fail," better to try and fail than to sit idle and do nothing. On the surface you might say that in either scenario nothing is achieved. On the surface level, I might agree with you.

However, there is a valuable lesson hidden just below the surface that is paramount that you learn. Even in failure, there are lessons learned that may not be able to be learned any other way than to fail. It may be this very lesson that you need to learn first before you can ever hope to realize your dreams. A-ha! A whole new perspective, is it not? See, this is just one reason why we who face adversity need a mentor or some other source we can draw from and learn lessons that can save us time and heartache. Failure is a part of life, but it is not the end. Most times failure is the only teacher we can learn from. It is failure that at times is actually little more than a stepping stone to the next lesson, the next piece of knowledge gained, the next piece of the puzzle we need, the next connection with another human that finally brings us to the place where our gifts can finally shine! Make no mistake about it, we all have gifts. Even the most profoundly disabled among us have much to offer. Whether they, or we, realize it or not they are or at least should be an inspiration to us all. You can argue with me until you are blue in the face, and I welcome the challenge, but I cannot be moved on this idea that everyone in this world has beautiful gifts within them.

Once you get over the "what if I fail?" hurdle, you have nothing but opportunities ahead of you. Sure, there will be times when you trip and fall. So what? Get up and keep going. You will undoubtedly encounter trees with low lying fruit you can pluck off and savor. Other fruit will not be so easy to access. Some fruit will be in front of you, ripe and ready to taste, however, it may be out of reach. No matter how out of reach it appears, it may present new challenges you hadn't thought of before. Maybe the obvious first thought of climbing the tree isn't the smartest way to get there. Maybe the fruit is too far out on a thin branch. Maybe a ladder might be more appropriate, but the ground under the fruit is too soft and unstable for a ladder.
Tricky stuff sometimes! And this is the fruit just barely out of your reach, I'm not even talking about that luscious ripe, fruit way up top yet!

What is the difference maker in the fruit tree scenario I just gave you? It may not be the obvious. It may not have anything to do with the height of the tree or tools available to you at the moment. It may not have anything to do with the people you have with you that can help you. Perhaps the difference maker is the answer to the following question. How hungry are you? You see, the real deciding factor is just that, how hungry are you? A man standing beneath a beautiful tree full of fruit, ripe and ready to be eaten, but out of reach, has to ask himself a question. How hungry am I? If the man decides, well, I just had breakfast, I'm not really all that hungry. Sure I could eat, but I am not willing to go through the trouble of getting to the fruit. My level of hunger is not sufficient to go through the work necessary and besides, it is not worth the risk. What if I fall? What if I get hurt, then what? The "what if" monster will eat this guy alive and he will never taste of the fruit. All things being equal, if this same man stands beneath the same tree and is hungry beyond belief, we will see a much different scenario play out. Even a man

weakened by prolonged hunger who finds
himself in this situation will act! Even if he
fails at first and falls. Even if he gets hurt, he
will get up again and again, trying different
ways if necessary to get what he wants, needs
and must have. We may even see ingenuity
come alive within him. We may see him shake
off pride and strip down to his underpants so
that he can tie his shirt and pants together in
order to have something long enough he can
swat at the fruit and knock it off its branch!
Problem solved, first bit of success realized.
Now the good carbohydrates and hydration
ingested from this amazing victory in the
man's life now strengthens him and causes
him to seek more fruit and take more action to
grab hold of more victories. With each victory,
the man climbs higher and higher growing in
health and strength all along the way.

Will the man reach the top? Does he get the
ultimate piece of prized fruit high atop the
tree? It is anybody's guess. We don't know the
answer. All we can do is sit back and watch
and route him on. The bottom line is whether

or not the man gets the ultimate prize or not, he has achieved far greater reward than the first man who allowed fear and the inability to take action ever realized. Maybe accessing fruit only halfway up the tree was indeed this particular man's full potential? Who is to say? I promise you this, the second man in this little mental exercise is happier, healthier and overall more satisfied than the first man probably ever will be. At least, until the first man understands the value of taking risk and stepping out and taking action.

Knowing what you now know, what man are you going to be? I guess it depends on how hungry you are.

Do whatever it takes to get yourself in a place where you are hungry enough. You simply must take action. You cannot afford to remain inactive. Enough hunger in your life can squash your fears, at least long enough to take your first steps and get a taste of your first small successes. Target fear and the "what if monster" and go after them. Become an excuse assassin yourself! Just because I may have coined the phrase and maybe by the time you read this I will have become known far and wide as THE Excuse Assassin does not mean you cannot become a great one, too! We all have our own, unique theater of operation. I do not live in your skin, and you do not live in mine. I can no more fight your battles for you than you can fight mine for me. You have been given your orders. You have been briefed on the enemies and their tactics. You have long ago been assigned your own personal theater of operation. You have now been more fully-armed, equipped and trained to go out there, destroy the enemy that holds you back from reaching your full potential. Now take action, soldier! Get out there and get the job done. I believe in you!

My Ultimate Secret Weapon

I am so excited and, honestly, a little bit sad at the same time. I am so excited for the fact that you have made it all the way through to the last chapter. I'm excited knowing that you are now equipped and far better prepared to face and overcome whatever challenge life has thrown your way, and whatever it may throw your way in the future. There is a level of excitement that I feel as well for coming so far myself with this project and reaching the final chapter is akin to being a few yards away from the finish line! I don't know about you but I'm ready for the juice and cookies! I've actually never ran a race, do they actually do that? The touch of sadness comes in when I think about the fact that momentarily I'll have to shut things down and turn my baby over to the editor for revision, proofreading and submission for distribution. Along with the joy of completion is a bit of sadness and a little "now what?" setting in. Don't worry about me, I'll rest a few days, regroup and zero in on the next task at hand.

In this chapter, I'm going to go more fully into what I consider my ultimate secret weapon. I have touched on it from time to time throughout the book, but have not made it a prominent part of my writing thus far. In a sense, it is because I did not want this book to get pigeonholed into a certain category. My purpose for the book as a whole is to share my personal life experiences, the challenges I have and am currently facing, and how I have overcome them and the lessons learned. I am pretty sure I said it early on, but it bears repeating. I determined long ago that I have not endured all this mess in my life for nothing. Somebody is going to get something out of all my struggles! I mean that most sincerely. I hope that everything I have shared with you is taken to heart, applied and becomes profitable to you, and not just in the   financial sense. I really hope that my life and my book serve you well and that you are truly better off because you invested the time to read this. I hope you have been inspired and motivated and are chomping at the bit to go get to work!

Besides all that, I feel certain matters are more personal in nature and best saved until there is relationship. Hopefully, now that you know me pretty well, in fact, probably better than some of my neighbors, you hopefully feel I have earned your trust.

So, I hope that this is the case and now as I move forward to share my ultimate and personal secret, I hope you will continue to hear me out and as with the previous five chapters, learn and apply what wisdom you glean henceforth.

I am often humbled when people sing my praises and tell me how much I inspire them. It is a weird thing for me. It is weird because I really believe in my heart that I am nobody special. I'm just a regular Joe, or Jeff, in my case! It is true that I have had to wrestle with some extraordinary situations in my time on this planet. True, at times it has been further intensified by the fact that trauma was piled upon trauma simultaneously, but there are really only two things I can attribute any successes I have had to. If anything, I can take credit for, and I hesitate to even do this, but it would have to be that I am pretty stubborn, and refuse to give up. Some would argue that is not an asset but a liability in that they may say I am not smart enough to know when to walk away. It might be a semi-fair argument! But my ultimate source of all my strength is, and always has been found in the person of my Savior, Yeshua (Jesus the Messiah).

You see, if you strip Him away from me and all that is left is me, what would be left? Well, I'd be an average Joe still, but I would be one who had no hope. Not only would I be void of hope, but also of any true purpose. What meaning would there be? If all life was was a series of days linked together that amounted to nothing, and then you die, how sad! All my trials with blindness, cancer, heart problems and so on would have no meaning or purpose. There would be no value in my life, or anyone else's for that matter.

Since I discovered and embraced Yeshua and his teachings, my spiritual eyes have been opened. Sure, in the physical I don't see much anymore that is terribly useful. Interestingly enough, the blessing in disguise which was hidden in the loss of sight resulted in me seeking His face all the more as I could no longer see my own. Naturally, I would love to have full sight restored. Don't think for a moment that I don't desire that, because I do more than I can express. However, I would not trade what I can see in the spiritual realm for anything that can be seen in the physical. There is no deal!

It is important for me to show you here that this relationship with Yeshua I am talking about isn't a club kind of thing. It is not about joining a church. It is not even much to do with calling yourself a Christian. It goes so much deeper than that.

What am I talking about? It is really hard for me to share this in short format. So, I think the best way I can do this is to let the Scripture speak for itself. I mean the entirety of the Word goes back thousands of years, all the way back to Torah on Mount Sinai.

The bottom line for me is that following the ways of the Messiah, Yeshua, is a lifestyle. It is one that does not just provide hope and peace of mind and wisdom and love for the here and now. Sure, it provides all that and so much more. Knowing in the here and now I can have comfort and assurance that the Almighty Creator has a plan and purpose for each of us and loves us so much he went to such extreme lengths to let us know how much we are loved provides me literally with infinite hope, comfort and   assurance.

In the most basic of terms, He (Yeshua) paid once and for all with his own blood to atone for my sins. What is sin? By definition it is a transgression of His law (Torah). Yeshua said, if you love me, DO my commands. All throughout history nobody had ever lead a perfect sinless life until Jesus lived out all 613 of the commandments. Yeah, I know you thought there were only ten. Those were essentially the table of contents. This sin I'm talking about, our basic human state, whether we want to be that way or not, cuts us off from Heaven.

G-d is Holy and cannot allow sin into his presence without it destroying us! By the way, that is not a typo. I deliberately removed the vowel from G-d. Why? Long story, but suffice it to say, it has to do with obeying the command to not desecrate the name. Also, I want everyone to read this. Jewish people who are Orthodox would stop reading immediately if they saw the vowel in there. So out of respect for the Word, and for my Jewish friends, I eliminate the vowel there.

So, let's see what the Rabbi Sha'ul (Apostle Paul) had to say on the matter of salvation and relationship to G-d's only son, Jesus (Yeshua in the Hebrew).

First, we need to deal with the fact that none of us are good enough all by ourselves. We cannot enter heaven because of any of our own merits. Romans 3:10, "as it is written, There is none righteous, not even one."(NASB) Again, addressing the idea that none of us are without sin, Romans 3:23 says, "for all have sinned and fall short of the glory of G-d." So, ok, once we see that we are in trouble and we are not keepers of His commands, but, in fact, are sinners, or ones who break his commands, what is the penalty for such things? Romans 6:23 has the answer, "For the wages of sin is death, but the free gift of G-d is eternal life in Christ Jesus our L-rd." Romans 5:8-10 "But G-d demonstrates His own love towards us, in that while we were yet sinners, Christ died for us... For if while we were enemies we were reconciled to G-d through the death of His Son, much more, having been reconciled we shall be saved by His life." So if Yeshua paid for my sins with his own blood because as Hebrews teaches, without the shedding of blood there is no remission of sin, how do we access that forgiveness? Romans 10:9-10, "that if you confess with your mouth Jesus as L-rd and believe in your heart that G-d raised Him from the dead, you will be saved; for with the heart a person believes, resulting in righteousness, and with the mouth he confesses, resulting in salvation."   Romans 5:1-2, "Therefore, having been justified by faith, we have peace with G-d through our L-rd Jesus Christ, through whom also we have obtained our introduction by faith into this grace in which we stand; and we exalt in hope of the glory of G-d."

Hopefully, the above arrangement of these verses paints a very clear picture for you. We need Yeshua. Three very simple words. simple but beyond my ability to provide enough emphasis as to how important they are. Does praying for forgiveness and accepting Yeshua as your personal Savior magically make everything better? In things eternal, yes! Immediately and forever they will be inexplicably better. Does that mean in this life things magically get better? Not necessarily. Sometimes certain aspects of our lives improve and get better. But we are not promised riches and a problem-free life, no matter what some prosperity-types try to teach. Remember, I shared the importance of vision and goals? Never, ever trade eternity for the here and now. The temporal world we live in is fleeting and passes before we know it. What we do in and for Jesus will last eternally. Set your goals on things eternal!

If this resonates with you and you want to make confession that Yeshua is L-rd and personally accept his sacrifice for your sins, then I invite you to pray the following prayer. If you are not ready or interested, you can still read it to see what is involved or you can check out. The choice is yours. Just remember, deciding to not make a decision is indeed a decision. It is called rejection. I pray that is not your choice.

Now if you are still with me and want to tap into my ultimate secret weapon and adopt it as your own, and of course I'm talking about having Yeshua as your own personal Savior and having Him to be your source of strength, then pray this prayer. It is not magic, but it is simple and profoundly powerful if you can say the following in all sincerity.

"Father, I acknowledge that I am a sinner. I have not kept all your commands and am guilty and worthy of the penalty of eternal death. I understand that you provided the perfect blood sacrifice in the giving of your Son, Yeshua. Through his death, burial and resurrection, it is now possible for me to have Him be my personal blood sacrifice, once and for all. Please forgive me and cleanse me of all my sins through His atoning blood. Make me new in your sight. Teach me your ways that I may be pleasing in your sight. I ask all this in the name of your Son, Yeshua. Amen!"

If you prayed that prayer and meant it sincerely, I can assure you that you are indeed saved and now belong to G-d! What now? This is just the beginning step of a journey that will hopefully last the rest of your life. Get yourself a Bible and begin to read it. Pray before each time you read and ask G-d to teach you His ways as you read, and His Holy Spirit will help you. Also, you need to plug into a community of believers and learn and grow with them. Pray G-d will show you the place He wants you to be connected. In the notes section at the end of the book, I will include some of my favorite Bible versions for you to check out, some of them are online and FREE! If you want further assistance in finding a church home that teaches the Word of G-d the way it was originally taught by the first century believers, then email me and I will help you to locate a congregation in your area.

Now how does all this fit together? Well, your eternal soul is secure if you sincerely prayed with me. As for the here and now, it will prove to be your ultimate source of strength. I don't care what obstacles you face. You will still have obstacles in all likelihood; you will now walk through them with the understanding that you are not alone. The G-d that created you now resides in you! You can handle all things! Why? The Word says we can do all things through Messiah Yeshua who strengthens us (paraphrased).

End Notes & Resources

The following are resources and contact information that will assist you further in your endeavor to became all you were meant to be!

Get a copy of my paperback book, "Power In Perseverance" TODAY!: www.jeffgrillo.com/products.html

My Personal email: jeff@jeffgrillo.com
Website: www.jeffgrillo.com
Blog: www.throttleupradio.wordpress.com
Podcast: www.jeffgrillo.com/audio.html
YouTube Channel: https://youtu.be/YamzUDTAj1w

Holy Bible (New American Standard Bible) Copyright 1997 Published by Foundation Publications

Many FREE Bible versions and additional study material is found at www.blb.org (Blue Letter Bible)

Epilogue

Moving forward, I have great expectations for you, the "Throttle Up!" network, and for what I intend to continue to do.

I look forward to hearing from some of you how this book and the network have impacted your life in a positive way.   I believe the things you will be able to do will blow you away.As you move into the fulfillment of your purpose and destiny, I know that the lives affected with positive change will go far beyond you, my readers, and touch the lives of many around you.

I believe that the numbers of people tapping into the blog, podcast and YouTube channel I have put together will continue to grow, and at some point the growth will be exponential.
I know that the impact that all of these posts will have will be of great value to all of those seeking help and change. I am certain that the quality of both the content and quality of production will continue to improve and

perhaps even be quite impressive to all who read, listen and watch.

I believe that the experience of building this community will continue to expand my horizons and grow me personally as I endeavor to serve those whom are drawn to my message. I know that the stories that you share back with me will bless me beyond my ability to put into words. I know that this return encouragement will only propel me to greater things and more innovative ways to reach out to you and new audiences.   I know that as I continue to speak before groups that the personal interaction that happens there will also continue to touch lives and yes, even motivate me to do more and more for those of you who place your trust in me.   To those of you who look to me as an example for inspiration and encouragement, I owe you a high-level of integrity, quality and accuracy of information that I impart to you.

The future, I believe, is bright. Even in the midst of upheaval and colossal world changes and dilemmas, I know that life goes on. I know that even in the midst of trials and turmoil the opportunity exists for positive change, growth, and even the possibility of turning things around and receiving the Mercy of G-d.

See 1 Chronicles 7:14 and following.
I believe that great things are possible and that you, regardless of what you face, can do things that will amaze you!

I pray the richest of blessings upon you. I pray you find your purpose

73511097R00063

Made in the USA
Columbia, SC
04 September 2019